T0146635

GENIUS
INVISIBLE
WALL

GIFTED CHILD

authorHOUSE®

AuthorHouse™
1663 Liberty Drive
Bloomington, IN 47403
www.authorhouse.com
Phone: 1 (800) 839-8640

Published by AuthorHouse 09/12/2017

ISBN: 978-1-5462-0540-1 (sc)
ISBN: 978-1-5462-0539-5 (e)

Library of Congress Control Number: 2017912990

Print information available on the last page.

Any people depicted in stock imagery provided by Thinkstock are models, and such images are being used for illustrative purposes only. Certain stock imagery © Thinkstock.

This book is printed on acid-free paper.

Paulette Lewis Brown with her only child Edgar.
A Genius in College. A mother knows best.

ACKNOWLEDGMENT

This book could not be written without the love and encouragement from my only Son Edgar and my best friend Ralph. My Church family plays a special song in my Heart. My Jamaican family uplifts my first story. Special thanks to my Mentor Dr Lionel V Mangue and my brother Solomon my Two Guardian Angels in Heaven. Peace and Love from America floating to Jamaica.

-Genius Invisible Wall.

INTRODUCTION

An Earth Angel explore an Avenue, writing is a way of life, it's like a Paradise of pure drinking Spring water. Sending my love in a selfie frame of mind. Genius invisible Wall. An open book to give you a brain freeze spasm. When the light bulb burst in the mind of a neglected child, the world mourn the loss of the unknown. Keeping the innocent in a safe haven of love. Cuddle with the king of the Castle. Breath of fresh air circles to find a source. A place to call home. When the candle lit and the smell of lavender covered the room, every tender heart breaks wide open for a view. Exposing the innocent to suspense. Love! what is love, why true love didn't showed up at birth.

This voice lingers with a child that never sleeps. Searching the world to find the father that never created a bond. Earth Angel begins to bond with Nature through Faith. Her Mother humming her way to the future. Broken Heart took away her voice.

Everyone is a Guessing factor. Trust is not a common ground, now leave Faith to nurture this wound forever. Escape to find that the World is not really round. It's cock eyed, and slightly off balance. The rest of this Journey, Jesus is a true comforter and a best friend. Soul searching, peace of mind will carry the gift of giving. A neglected and poor child with eyes set on America is all grown up with a dream to change the world. with a gifted Spirit. Searching every extraordinary Valley for a soul mate, with an Invisible wall, only one can see. Smile if you can view the direction of an Earth Angel Invisible Wall. We might need a Genius with a doctors degree to set you free. A helping hand is a cool breeze. Explore, say hi when you can see me.

CHAPTER 1

The Core of every household is love. A family so broken with family drama. One parent home, Faith, food and shelter is an open book across the Border. A step-father volunteer to share the burden of having step children. Faith stands in the form of prayers. Life was tough for a child that was different. Hiding behind the wall at the church for cover was a mother. Humming her soul away. Hurt by everyone she ever dated, she share one advice, never trust a man in this world of pain. Jamaica out of many, we're one. sets in the mind of a gifted child. Life must go on.

School is a long walk without water, a sandwich for lunch and a group of community kids wonder without hope, hunger is a daily Ritual, yet it could be a fasting Recipe. The one good thing everyone could still practice how to smile. Pain from poverty rarely cripple the poor man child. Education struggles to come through, perseverance lingers and strengthen ones Soul. Fight the good fight. The golden road, leads to the city. Now it's time to find a family member to turn on the switch to the future. Feeling lost without a brother who was killed by a drunk driver. Life for the Earth Angel feels like a Hurricane.

Gilbert disaster ready to quit and turn over a new page. Life wasn't easy in the Country.

This family drifts apart, a brother who went to Heaven way too early visits in a dream bond with Nature my sister. A step father went away on Farm Working, never returns. Poor Gifted child plays with the rest of her siblings, but it never feels the same. Remember fishing and playing in the Rain was a bond and memory, a promise game played by two. Now the future looks dim, with uncertainty, all eyes sets on Kingston City. Church was every Sunday everyone has to attend. If not, chores would feel like a hell bound. chopping woods and cutting grass and feeding Goats. Chickens and Pigs, a family legacy. The Sun and Moon was two of A favorite pass time for neighborhood kids. Everyone would look forward to Nature. Little gifted Earth Angel rarely speaks. A inner Voice paved the way with a glimpse into the future.

An older sister got married and is now a Pastors wife. She never looks back. Family to her was not a poor mother who rarely speaks, or two brothers who can hardly read. A gifted sister who always wants to be alone. Her new family took president over her every being. Everyone knows that love will someday show in every corner of this household. one gifted child would say out loud for everyone to hear. I will bond with Nature, I will bond with Nature. The Birds needs food and water. keep the Trees fresh and Green. Don't forsake the Ocean. Smile with the Sun, Moon and Stars. I will Bond with Nature for the rest of my life. Then take a stand and remember my brother Solomon. He'll forever hold our hands when in sorrows. After High school the gifted child sets eyes on Moving to Kingston for a better life with her Auntie. This life must come to an end. Poverty was more than enough for one family. God guidance sets in motion, complete research for a better life straight ahead. A glimpse of the City life.

CHAPTER 2

At this point it should be clear by now that I am the Gifted child. With my mind set in high gear. I kiss my family goodbye. Wave to all my neighbors and friends. Also find time to hug my two Mango Trees. A few friends were in tears, I try to hold a Brave face to keep my company on the Bus. My Faith walk me to the Bus stop, I could see Jesus face, guiding me to be a Legacy in the Future. Kingston City will curve the Heart of the gifted child. Nature wild and free. I was thinking very deep on the Bus Ride, very loud Reggae music for company. Loud Jamaican Patios in every seat. One Lady even offer me something to eat. I said no thanks then went to sleep. The horn went off on the bus. This was the final Stop.

My Aunt was waiting at the Bus Stop with open arm. I felt like a little Mary Lue, Nick name for frighten Friday. Her smile was larger that life itself. She looks very happy to see me. I know that I could trust my Father's sister, she knows her brother wasn't there for me. So she wants to make up for borrowed time. She took me home, where her husband and her two daughters awaits my arrival. To my surprise, they were poorer than my mother. They were also trying to make ends meet in the City. I felt guilty. Maybe I should stay in the Country with my immediate family. They convince me to think Positive and just live for the moment. Eat and feel free. Faith, food and shelter is all people really need. My eyes was wide open, I said what about money? My Aunt said Money don't grow on Trees. Everyone has chores around here, including you. I said no problem.

My goal was to get a job of any kind, I was 18 yrs old with no experience, just bright eyes, and a big smile. My prayer was a daily bread, I really ask God to send me to College. The first in my family Tree. This would make history, if I have a College Degree. At this point I have not money, just a plan in place, I feel like a Suspense Zone, with a poor Banner hanging from my mindset. Impossible to be me, I must say I did have Twenty Dollars to my name. Food and shelter was already provided. Church was every Sunday. I Prayer Base gets stronger, everyone in the Church cover me in prayer. I feel safe with a Goal in mind. Please help me Jesus to survive this Journey with very little money to keep me focus on this Journey.

One Monday the the light Bulb lights up, when I catch the Flu, for some reason I wasn't feeling very sick, but my Aunt took me to the Neighborhood Doctor for a check up. This could be a clue. She gave me Fifty Dollars, way less that the office visit. My name was called, the door open wide, a very tall Chinese Doctor appears out of nowhere, I personally never seen a tall Chinese before. His demeanor was very welcoming. I started coughing, he took one look at me, and said my Dear the Flu is going around, and your'e no exception to the rule. It found you too. He said I am going to start you out with some cough Medicine for free.

Keep the Fifty dollars your Aunt gave you. My fee is four times this amount. I can see that you just move from the Country, what's your next move, my eyes sparkle with joy. I just started talking. The most I have spoken in years.Well I would love to go to College and get a degree, But at this point I have no Job for support financially. Deep in my Soul I just feel like I could someday afford College. This total stranger of a Doctor gave me a Research. Here is my Business Card. Find the best College around here, or a University. Choose one then come back to me. If your'e going to study you also have to be in a safe and quiet environment. Shop around for secured Apartment. Come back and see me with your findings. I know almost everyone in this City. Just call my name everywhere you go for a test.

To cut a long story short, I call and return with my findings to the Doctors Office. I calculate my monthly expense. To my surprise, he pays My College and New Apartment Rent for one year. I almost fainted. I look up the Sky and Jesus was smiling. He said it's okay my child, I guided you here. Enjoy your study, compliment from me. One day later I was given a new Car to drive to College. The owner of the nearest Supermarket, brought me my grocery every Saturday. My Aunt still couldn't believe her ears. My mother in the Country didn't believe a thing. I was in a gated Apt, with mostly students. I became friends with a few. After a year of study, my Doctor Earth Angel became my best friend. He taught me how to meditate and separate from stress. In my eyes, he was the best. Great Advice from his Gifted Soul.

I did great in College, then landed a Job at the Bank, I was so please with my achievements, I always help everyone in my family Tree. Thanks to Dr Mangue. Everything was going great. After ten years of an open book, A sheltered Bird, needs to fly and smell the Roses. if you love someone set her free, if they returns, then it was meant to be. By now I call Dr Mangue my Mentor. His words meant a lot to me. So I follow his encouragements to the future. He said, someday my Health will fail me even though I am a doctor. I know your Heart will never be the same. Set your sight on America. Stay Focus, continue to Meditate and Pray. call me everyday. My Heart aches too. Believe it when I say to you. Forever we will be more than friends. Even when I am long gone, my Heart will beat for you in Heaven. Keep your circle small, still make a few friends. I will always be with you. Call me everyday collect from American. Think of this for your next journey. Explore Nature and feel free.

CHAPTER 3

Stepping into my new shoes, in the Heart of America. Feeling like a new Queen from the Soul of Jamaica. Still thinking that a better life here is a poor man game. My Roots will always be a Paradise to me. Traveling to another Country is always temporary breeze. As you can see I will always bond with Nature. My Mentor will always be my Primary Doctor, even if God take him a away early. His advice to me, My dear, take notes, I won't be around forever, it worries me that you receive no love from your real Father. Your ability to make it here in Jamaica will be challenged, if I am not around. Keep Healthy, monitor your weight, every headache is associated with Blood Pressure. Give more than you receive. Keep a small circle of friends. Remember everyone birthday. Whatever challenge cross your path, I expected you to carry on. MVP is a Gifted Spirit not a Diagnosis. Learn to give not Borrow or lend. Leave all Stress to fend for themselves, open no room to stress cells. First note, True love never dies. You will be my Earth Angel forever. The only one I ever trusted. The poorest true best friend. I send to College. My gift to you.

This chapter is filled with advice from my Mentor, the smartest Chinese Doctor that lives in Jamaica. He helps so many people, but I can only speak for me. Is humble spirit Bonded with mine. His pass life was not my business, I ask very little of his life. I only know what he told. If he lied at this point nothing matters, I can only see good in everyone. He was all I know, when true love shows its face in my life. My mother was so silent, I know she was hiding something, so she didn't talk much about my father, okay that line came out of nowhere. I must get back on track. Back to my Mentor best attribute I would give you the World, but you never ask for anything. the most important request was to graduate College. I guide you along when you visited the Office, I introduce the medical field to you like a student intern. My method will carry on in your Brain forever. I feel obligated to always see you through. I will continue until I can no longer. Now ten years later, your'e stronger than they think. Take couple more trips to America then decide on your new life. I will still be your second Rock, Your Faith is always first. When I get to Heaven, I will be your Wings on Earth, Smile.

Here's a financial dose of my Kindness, use it PRN. Thanks for being my best friend all these years. We will have a forever Bond. I wish I could tell my grown up children. But it's okay, my way my actions are mine to keep. Regret is no secret. Everything between us was a gift send from a higher Power, we cannot explain without a microscope with the stethoscope right next to it. Only God knows, the accuracy of the future, mankind will dibble and dabble to feel younger. Smile to the unknown. We enjoy each other company with no question sign, we carry this Journey with a straight line. We cross paths in silence. Your safety was always my intention. A gifted friend who has never failed me.

Your Phone calls will always be collected, your welfare is always Safety. Humble yourself in your circle. Be aware, be alert, be on top of things that will affect your ability to think. Use your wise buds, they grow from Trees. Smile when you think of me. I could be your Chinese Palm Tree.

Kick in Nature from time to time, walk the Ocean, sing a song from me. I am everything you are because, I love me. Funny way to think. Just see me. I will be there.

Life in America will not be easy, Know the real from the fake, but say nothing, Compliment all without judgment. Stay away from gossip, that's the poison that's eating the Heart of Americans. Stay focus and stay Low. You will always be my assistance, Allow no one to cripple your soul or give you a collapse lungs. Just life and love freely. Your Heart will guide you to true love in America. It's very hard to find the right Valve that will open with honesty. Smile forever, put that Velvet Teddy Bear in the closet. Most memorable birthday gift. someday cut it open for an even bigger surprise.

I remember when I gave you that Birthday gift, your eyes lights up like a Christmas Tree, when you see the size. Fun memories. Meditation was one key to our happiness. Silence is golden with a young Caribbean Jamaican Queen. I know this reader is thinking way beyond this page.

Anyway this is my prescription for you, Happiness is first, money alone will not cut it. Love is a daily bread, Faith will uplift it. Meditation is your strength more is better than enough. Peace, no one can buy Peace you have to find it within. Allow no man to use you. Know the sign, I shared enough wisdom to last for a lifetime Movie. Call on me everyday, Hope to see you again. My Heart will always beats love for you. My daily emotion Pill. Right now Jamaica is loosing my best friend. A country girl was my right Wing. Forever bonded in complete silence.

CHAPTER 4

When I stepped off the plane in America, I was just a visitor with a small suite Case with two weeks of clothes and a very large Teddy Bear for a happy memory note. My Visa was for ten years, so the immigration Officer didn't ask much question when he saw who my Mentor was. He gave a letter, just in case of any hassle. I was ask to throw away my Mangoes but I was okay with that. I must say, America is the most beautiful Country in the World, I feel like I was going to learn so much in this Country. I was fascinated by lights, so much lights, everywhere I go. Jamaica was like a Flash light, now America is the King and Queen of lights, whatever that means. I was happy to see, my life lights up to new Diversity. Yes the simple things fascinates me. Everyone has an accent to me, people compliment me on my Jamaican Accent often enough. Patois is my English. Sorry please don't expect this book to be in perfect English. It would never be written by me. Now lets move right along, Outside waiting in the very crowded area was my stepfather who help to raised me in Jamaica, and his new wife. I feel welcome by both. all roads leads to New Jersey. The ride home was a little awkward

I haven't see my step father in Ten Years. He never return from Farm working, He wasn't there when I graduated College. So a lot was on my mind. I was meeting his wife for the first time. She was a Christian so I feel safe with her. All she talk about was taking me to Church, where my Step father was a Deacon.

My eyes and mind was in high gear, trying to process what my Mentor told me about Survival in America. First my dear you have to get Certified in the Medical field, start at the shortest course then work your way up. So the first six weeks Certificate, I accomplish was Certified home health Aide, Then I went for Certified Nurses Assistance. Both courses was like a piece of Cake base on what I already know from Dr Mangue. I was like a little Minnie him at his office, 1 Regal Plaza Kingston. Bunny was also his right hand help, in the Office. My next step was finding a job in Healthcare. I settled in with the most wonderful family in the World. The Mounts family was so welcoming. I took care of Dorothy who is now a Guardian Angel, Everyone was very nice and caring. Every weekend I would go home and go to Church with my Step Father and his wife Evelyn. I was appreciative of their help. I just wish my brothers were here. But I rarely talk about it with my step father. He said his wife would help him to get his children over here, but it never happen. Only God knows why. I can only pray and thank God that he gave me a free pass to come to America. I just love the smell of Nature. It was everywhere. Birds, Oak Trees, Ocean, a lot of Farm Lands. Everything a poor Country girl would cherish. I did walk a lot by myself. I love to talk with Jesus on my long walks. He always assure me that he was always by my side. in the World that my Creator built, he didn't waste any time to find me a Husband, After six months in the Country, out of no where the dating scene sends someone very single my way. We wasn't very compatible, but were very single, and ready to mingle. I was new from Jamaica, He Just moved from Detroit Michigan, into his new career, a Prosthetic Technician. I was a live in Aide. He use to waste his time correcting my English, I could see the pain on his face when I speak in my Jamaican Patois. I use to drive him crazy when I didn't try to speak proper. Oh that was so funny to me. After one year with my Patient she Expired to her home in the sky. Heaven Gates welcome her home. After just dating six months. I was pregnant, with my pride and Joy. I was excited when I was told that we were having a boy, I shout out loud thank you Jesus. Immediately after that we got Married. I was already three Months Pregnant. I trust God that this Union would last. But he has other plans for both of us. Don't change yourself to be someone else. Just be there for your son. Jesus whisper to me.

I gave birth at Princeton University Hospital, where I was also an Employee. I was in labor for twenty four hours. I was a mess, my husband was there, of which I was grateful. November 26, 1996 the best thanksgiving gift I ever received. I know Jesus loves me. Little Edgar came into the World without making a sound, the cord was wrapped around his neck, I could feel my lungs collapsing, please Lord save my son. When I heard his voice, I feel like my entire World begins on that date. I couldn't believe I was a Mom, I was crying for a very long time, My husband was in tears too. He went down stairs and brought me Flowers. My step Father and his wife was outside in the waiting room. Everyone was over joyed. I was at Peace and needed some sleep.

After two days. it was time to take my Thanksgiving Gift home. Little Edgar was everything I was looking for. I never have to care for a little one like this before.

I was very careful with everything. Germs was first thing on my safety list, everyone have to wash their hands on the outside before entering the house.

I really didn't want to see anyone because extra weight took over my body. I wasn't feeling pretty. But my baby boy was everything. I forgot how to be a wife.

My focus was only on our Son. I really didn't want to put him down. He was always in my arms. I was addicted to this little precious Soul. I cannot explain.

I call my Best friend, my mentor Dr Mangue, I told him how I was feeling, He said please find time for yourself. This is not normal. put your son down breathe Being a new mother is not going to be easy. Just Meditate and breathe. I told him that my Husband was in his own world too. I could hear him on the phone with his family. I just have to stick around for my son. As soon as he knows me, this union is history. Deep down I felt the same way. His favorite line was, it's my way or the high way. I use to pray for that day to come. Anyway when I look at my son, he sends a zest for life running through my veins. He was full of of life. I would play with him daily. I feel like a child again. Only this time I have to take care of the child. I stayed on Maternity leave for six weeks, then it was time to return to the work force.

CHAPTER 5

Princeton University Hospital was a great place to work, I work as a Certified Phlebotomist for over seven years. After I gave birth to my Son

I changed from full time employee to a part time wanna be. My priority was to spend more time at home, so I could eliminate baby sitter need. my Husband works days, I work night. I was coming in, he was going out. Two people under one roof, providing for one child. I pray to God how long would this last. Everyone has needs. we just wasn't there emotionally for each other. No one taught us how to be a Married couple.

We try communicating, but he correct every line in one sentence. After awhile I just stop speaking to him. He was not a happy Husband, but he was the best Father. He focus totally on our son Edgar. They both share the same name and same birthday. They bonded like two peas in a Pod.

One of my daily chores, was to call Dr Mangue, I look forward to hear his voice. There was never a dull moment speaking to him on the phone.

He knows everything about me. I wouldn't change a thing about our friendship. God sends him in my life for a reason. I would never forget his kindness.

Before I close this Paragraph, I must say that my Husband did give me an ultimatum Stop talking to this so called friend of yours. or else, you will see.

That didn't sit too well in my mind, so I start hiding to make collect calls to Jamaica. It didn't cost me a thing to talk to my best friend. No one could stop our friendship. People always question our friendship in Jamaica, we would send them around in Circle. Two Minds thinks exactly alike.

Well at this point my Husband was getting very frustrated, our son was sleeping in the bed with us. This was my idea, I was to put him in his crib to sleep.

I didn't want him to die of SIDS, a complicated Crib disease. So I would sneak my Son out to sleep on my side of the bed. This was so unfair to my Husband

He use to complain to his mother, She used to tell him, pick your son up and bring him to the Crib yourself. He would listen to her until one day I fell asleep in the Crib with our Son. Yes it was that bad. I didn't want to loose the only family I really have in America. I pray to God daily, please Lord let me change. I need to be a good Wife and be with my husband. I think I was afraid to get pregnant again. Maybe that was the reason, I am not sure. All I think about was being a good mother for our son. I go to work at night, all I could think about was little Edgar. His daddy was great, I just think a child always need their mother more.

We continue like this for five years, back and forth to work, Two parent family with very little communication, when we do, it turns into an argument. We survive the best way we know how. Western Union was a regular from Jamaica. I was always grateful for Lionel Kindness. He meet our son one time, he fell in love with little Edgar. I never return to Jamaica from that one visit. Five more years passed.

Then I received that dreadful call. Dr Mangue passed away. I couldn't breathe, That's when I find out his real age. He never tell anyone his correct age. I never question what he told me. After all, it didn't matter. He was always there fore me. I cried for weeks, I couldn't attend his funeral. I prayed and ask him to forgive me. Jesus whisper to me. Don't worry he forgive you already. Just stay focus and be a good mother. I am with you always. Start praying daily again.

I mourned my best friend lost. I never stop missing him. but life must go on. He teaches me a lot about life. I feel like he was a Genius that nobody really knows he would give you everything and die a pauper if he could. Hope that line make some sense. By now my Marriage was on a downward spiral, we could never see eye to eye. Work was just work, no room for a raise. So I start looking in the paper for another Job closer to home. After a very long weekend arguing back and forth with Hubby number one. I finally decided that it's better going our separate ways. I moved into a low income apartment with our Son. My husband was very frustrated, he stays in the New Jersey a little while longer, then he transfer back to Detroit.

Our son was safe with me. I was feeling like a happy bunny. I just work full time, and stay focus. Everything was going great. My ex-husband pay his child support faithfully.

Little Edgar was doing good in School. Life was looking up. Except I still missed my best friend, my mentor Doctor Mangue. His name is going to be in this book a lot. So sorry if you're confused at this point. He once told me that I was a Genius. I believe his every word. I just didn't pay too much attention to it.

I Joined a single mom club, I happen to meet a few single mothers, everyone was on a different path. I attend for awhile then just stop going. I continue to pray everyday, I even teaches my son how to ask God for anything. So we use to pray together. I also teaches him Meditation. He didn't like that too much.

Life at this point to me was mother and son school more fun. My son was out going I was more reserved. I probably have only three close friends. Nature has brought me more gifts than mankind. I was always giving, especially on birthdays. Yet my birthday was always a silent zone. My immediate Jamaican family would even call me on my birthday and ask me to send them some Western Union money. Not even a birthday Card. Maybe two Cards in Twenty years. It's just funny to me, no problem was an emblem in our Country. Everyone was raised to say no problem man. So I have to over look, what true love really is.

Maybe remembering my birthday was not important. I always wish I could give everyone in the World a Birthday Gift. Maybe God will make this possible someday for me. At this point I wasn't going to Church, but I would pray everyday. I was very close to Jesus, When Dr Mangue died, I asked Jesus to be my best friend. I always talk to him. Sometimes I feel like I was living with Jesus and my Son. I used to feel very blessed. Peaceful, just complete silence, I would Meditate Daily. Walk to the Park, Talk with the Birds, enjoy Nature from every angle possible. My Son was a very popular child in school. He has a lot of friends I couldn't keep count. Sometimes I use to sneak up on them at the Park. He didn't like that too much. I talk to a couple boyfriends, I just couldn't feel that trust factor with anyone of them. They all disappoint me in the end. When I look up in the sky. Jesus said I told you so. I am your true best friend for life.

I went on couple Interviews, I needed a change and I needed a raise in pay. I was an ASCP Phlebotomist, I should be receiving much more base on my qualifications and experience. I was promised a Raise but It didn't come on time. Centra State Medical called me for an Interview. Two weeks later, I was offered a job. With a great package. Health Insurance and 401K I was excited for the future. My Son was happy with school all his friends were great kids.

I use to feed them all, when they come over. Just like my mother in Jamaica. She would feed the whole neighborhood if she could. My new job as a Phlebotomist was a dream come through. The Laboratory was divided at the get go.

Phlebotomist team, Hematology Dept, Chemistry Dept, Blood Bank, Microbiology, Histology, Cytology and the Morgue. Laboratory was very large. Mostly white employees. Fifteen Blacks employee was visible, They were on different shifts. One main Supervisor with many preceptors in every department. I never worry about the gossip in the Department. because I was certified in my field. I didn't pay much attention to gossip. I work to the best of my ability. Keep my in service up to date. Smile with everyone I meet. I really didn't see a problem until I notice that everyone that gets fired from this Department was black employee. I prayed to God this wasn't so. But everything was clear as daylight. This main Supervisor wasn't doing too great when it comes on to African American. It looks like she has a hatred towards that race. She would set employees up against each other then fire the Black employee, every time. I saw what was happening so I stay clear and give a blind eye to what was happening. To me it wasn't any of my business. So I think of my Roots, we were trained to mind our own business, stay away from mix up and blender.

This is call gossip. So I know how to skip around the trouble makers. I was always busy working. After work I would enjoy time with my son. I would tell him I love him everyday. He was my rock. I just could talk to my son about everything. I always pray for the people at work. It was a silent Zone, even though it was obvious that prejudice was a big factor in this Department for many years. I stayed focus, be nice with everyone, Jesus always tell me to pray, in complete silence, he would give me wings. So I was free as a bird, many times when others fight over minor things. My Faith was everything floating me away from their drama. After awhile I was watching from a distance. Total Hostile environment.

Things got so bad in the Laboratory, it was down to only five African American Phlebotomist, I was included. My supervisor would write me up on a daily Basis, Now I think it was my turn to go. She call me in her office everyday, wanting me to sign her complain about me. I promise her that I wouldn't sign her lies. This goes on for many more years, we were down to two African Americans, The other phlebotomist was apart of the game. They try to set us up everyday. Until one day my supervisor set up the other African American to provoke me. I was very aware of how the Laboratory runs so I was on the look out that day. Near the end of the shift, this employee out of nowhere came up to me, and said if you ever touch my patient label again, I am going to kill you. I was so shock I couldn't believe my ears. Everyone was looking to see if I would fight back, but I turned the other cheek. I could see the Main Supervisor who set this up, hiding in Blood Bank. I went in there to report the incident, She look surprise that I was threatened, but I know that she sets this up. She just didn't expect it to back fire. This employee was fired. I then went to Civil Rights and explain my eleven Years of torment. They took the case then accept Bribe from the Hospital. I know their Investigation was filled with holes. Money talks the poor man child walks. November 16th 2012 was the day Jesus took full control of my Career. He steps in and guide this journey. He helps me to heal from their critical criticism and lies. I never look back. This is my sixth Book. Jesus would come to me in my dreams. He wants me to never stop writing. Someday he wants me to tell my story in detail. But for now he wants me to write or the World. With over 12K followers on Twitter, Facebook friends looking forward to read my uplifting Post. Everything started to add up. Maybe these dreams are guiding me to write. I have no degree in writing Poetry. My English is considered broken, we call it Jamaican Patois. Nothing stop my progress. I even have more followers than my publisher, not to sound cocky, but I feel like a higher power is guiding my writing. I continue to pray everyday with my son. When I was alone I pray out loud to Jesus. By now I have a few fail relationships. I even have a miscarriage in the past. God way of saying, stop living in Sin. Stay on the right track with me. Serve only me. Watch all your dreams come through. I strengthen my Faith over the years. I then join a Pentecostal Church, I learn a lot in this Church. If your Tithe didn't look up to par. your'e just a number that would be beaten down by fake personalities. Smile I could survive in any environment. So I Continue to read the Bible the first book in my Heart.

CHAPTER 6

After many years of turmoil and pain on the job, I finally decided to volunteer as a New Jersey EMT. This was for the Community my way of saying God will survive somehow. I signed up with Princeton Hospital temp Agency for two year, I worked as a travelling aide. My one patient took me on vacation with her to Key West, that's when God open my eyes to research Florida. I know he has a plan somewhere in the works for me.

I went to sleep one night, and I woke up with the most memorable dream. My dear you will be the Author of many books. I will guide you along.

Don't worry about your Jamaican Slang. Write until eternity. Just do it for me. I know that was a heaven sent dream. So I never stop writing.

Today I am the Author of five poetry Books. I can't believe I could write this much. But I kept on going through hard times. Following my Faith.

I still go to church on Sunday, even though I know it was going to be temporary, I didn't feel at home in this Church. Gossip would tear the new members apart. No room for growth. One thing I learn that God will show up everywhere. So I live in peace that way. Smiling and waving to the outside world. deep inside was still missing my best friend Dr Mangue, from time to time he flashes in my mind. Maybe he's still alive. My thoughts wonders sometimes for a comfort Zone. I learn to keep the Faith and be strong. My Son graduated High school, I was so proud of him.

He then move to live with his dad to start College. We have that long talk, mother and son talk. Everything was great. I really misses him, but it was time for his father to chip in. Help him to grow into a productive man. I was deprived of that as a child, so I wouldn't put my son through the same Family History. He moved to Detroit Michigan, I stayed in New Jersey, volunteering to keep my mind open to the World. Then I worked part time to Survive.I know God has a better plan for me, so I let him lead me to the future.

My step father wife took sick, this was a very sad moment, she was given only six months to live. she was diagnose with Ovarian Cancer. The family was very distraught. We prayed together, cry together, she also hug me and said sorry if she didn't accept me as a step daughter, We hug each other and pray for healing. Her Doctor explain that her situation was getting worst, she lost her eye sight, Then she was placed on Hospice, everything was happening so fast my step father was at a lost. his Church members would take turn to visit. I was feeling very sad to see her health just went down hill.

One day I was sitting with Evelyn, she told me, that God wants me to meet her brother Ralph, when he travel from Florida. Please be here tomorrow.

I was present when Ralph drove from Florida to New Jersey all alone to visit his sister. He was crying when he saw her condition. She couldn't see but she could still speak. She held both of our hands together, she said my dear I know you for over twenty years, I never mention my brother, because I was married to your step father, but now Jesus is calling me home. He wants this to be a union. Give it time. Get to know each other. Let no one come between you both. You have my blessings. Ralph I am your sister Evelyn I will always love you. Forgive everyone, learn to carry on without me.

My step father was in tears, he was losing his best friend. I was in pain for him. I was feeling very helpless, everyone came to say their good byes.

One day I was at work, I got that dreadful phone call Evelyn pass peacefully at Home. She was a magnificent lady, full of life, I missed her dearly.

I spoke with her brother daily, he came to her Funeral, We were there for Papa, that's what I call my step father. I did my best to help in every way I could.

I worked for six more months, then set sail to Florida. Residing in one of Ralph Homes. Again another big step in my Faith. You can think otherwise, it's perfectly fine in my world.

I moved to Florida, challenge the CNA test past it immediately. Then I signed up with two Medical Agency. Ralph owns his business, so we saw each other when we could. We talk on the phone everyday. We could talk about anything. If it wasn't for her sister, we wouldn't know each other, we talk about that a lot.

I continue to pray everyday. One night I went to bed, I could hear clearly, you will Marry your best friend Ralph, allow no one to get between this Union. It might be Evelyn talking to me from her Grave. I Told Papa about the dream. He said my child. your husband will find you. I said to him, that's a poem I wrote in my book, things just sounds supernatural, but true from beyond the skies. I am experiencing dreams more often. Writing books like crazy. I just feel blessed. My Job was going great. I have an assignment every week. I joined a local Church, not much members, maybe thirty members, seven died in one year. I notice that five pastors was married to the same sex, I also notice that over the one year five Pastors preaches, all of them were Married to the same sex. I love them all the same, but I ask in a very important meeting, Just for the record, is this Church a Gay Church, could you make room for a straight Pastor sometimes.

There were complete silence. Anyway someone answer and said, I can't believe you ask such question. This must be the work of the devil. I said no it's not, Jesus wants me to ask in an open forum. If it's a Gay Church invite more Gays so they can have a place to worship. I stuck around few more weeks then I moved on. Jesus wants me to be happy in a

Pentecostal Church. But he wants the World to know that he loves everyone. Gay or straight. Pray one for another. Always put your faith first. Help each other in crisis. I say my goodbye and move on to the nearest Pentecostal Church.

I visited Trinity Church and I loved it. It was a Pentecostal worship Center, The Holy spirit was welcome here. I feel like a child again. This is how I was raised Everyone giving praises to God. I enjoy giving my offerings and meeting people with the same interest. Jesus first regardless of our Race. Life is everything beautiful, God is working out everything for me. My relationship with Ralph was almost perfect. I kept on writing, one night, I dream that I own the World Largest Poetry Workshop. Creative kids and Gifted Souls were all members. I woke up looking around in shock. So I wrote some unique poems about work shops for Jesus. Someday this dream will come through, I am just waiting for the right Mentor to come my way. Feel free to think about this open space.

Community Children escape route, peace for everyone. My Faith will forever guide this Journey. My son is doing great. My dog Molly is right here with me.

The Sun is out, The Palm Trees are swaying, Nature everywhere to read. Fun people doing their thing. God is still in control of my Writing. He's setting everything in motion.

CHAPTER 7

Working the night shift works perfectly for me. I have the most uplifting patient. She was one hundred years old.

Her sister was a very charming and powerful lady. Her motivation was beyond word. Never a dull moment. I admire the fact that my patient and her sister pray every day. This reminds me that Faith is always the strength that kept us going The Rosary beads with the Cross was always obvious at the bed side. Her sister would sit and read her favorite Poems and sing her favorite songs. I feel like I was at the right place at the right time. All Gods plan. I watch Aides and Certified Nursing Assistants come and go. But for some reason, I never leave. My patient was a past Nurse, she has done a lot of good to help others. My job is to provide the best comfort care in her time of need. I also assist her sister with my help. This is the most peaceful and quiet household I have ever worked in. I could see why God was sheltering me under his wings. I have been through a lot.

Without getting too personal, this job was made especially for me. Twelve hour shift was an extra Bonus from Heaven.

My Dream is to write as many books as my Faith would take me. I have no training in writing and this is my sixth book. My English is all over the place. It's based with Jamaican Patois. Just the way Jesus wants it. I am different, I will be the change the World is looking for. The Gifted souls of the Universe is given a bad rap. It's time that the way is clear as daylight. No more roadblocks and doubt standing in the way of the extraordinary ones. The more I worked with these two sisters, I realized that Jesus placed me with two Gifted Souls. We could talk about anything. I didn't have to struggle to fit in. They requested me for seven days. I could only work five. Everything in this house was Jesus first. I didn't talk about my Faith, they could tell that I was a christian. They said there's something about me, they just wish I was here years ago. I continue to provide the best comfort care possible. I stayed in my scope of practice. I remember everything my Mentor taught me. I document every interactions, any changes was well recorded on paper. I was schedule for two weeks. Seven months later I am still here.

The sister ask me something very personal. Tell me something Paulette, are you an Angel?. I smile for a peace of mind. God is good, he will never fail us. He knows us by name.

Some day my assignment will be Expired with with a new Angel in Heaven. A sister will mourn the loss. Her family and friends will be a helping hand.

I will give my farewell and love. My heart will ache, with a sign, don't get too personal is not real. I will continue to pray for this family to Heal.

My Hope is that the sister should never be alone for awhile. Just someone to talk to, will heal her wounds. This sister Bond was very real. I could see and feel the Love between them. Now an Angel in Heaven, sisters weeps. My next assignment will be part time. I will pursue my dreams. Reading poetry to uplift others. Poetry Workshops for our Gifted and Creative Souls. I will wait for my Faith to guide me. I cannot do this alone. Now my Marriage is going great, I am a newly wed with a goal in mind. Honey Moon will come one day. Right now we both have a busy schedule. Every weekend is our time together.

My son is doing excellent in College. I am so proud him. We talk almost everyday on the phone. He's my heartbeat love song. God has been very good to my family. I never doubt his will for my broken family tree. I feel sometimes that my real father someday will have a lot of explaining to do. In the same breath as I got older. I realizes that my mother will have the same amount of explaining to do in the future. I am a family secret, will be a suspense Zone for this time around. I love to keep you guessing. Genius invisible wall is a vast Ray of Sunshine. Only the Gifted can see beyond the Rays. Hmm your'e in deep thoughts.

Stay this way until the end of the Chapter.

Everyone will have a different opinion of this Title. Whatever you bring to this table, Please feel free to express yourself. Someday my Workshops will find the answer to many questions in the World. Our Journey is different, yet our Hearts could afford to be at the same place today. Feel it right now, it's beating Not every beat is normal. See our Journey as a learning experience. Find Peace and Love in the same room. Leave doubt at the door. Someday we might need it to answer why. The goal is to help everyone with an open mind. Genius Invisible Wall will be an open Book. We will see things from different Angles.

We will ask questions that will take me for a loop. Smile in every moment. Every corner is worth pursuing. Working the night shift is still an ongoing project

Until a full understanding of a new Career kicks in. Now I must say the sound of thunder Roars, It's Raining all day. Nature is telling me a story. Not yet to be Revealed. Pray for everyone in the World. Pray for healing, pray for Success, pray for true Love in every Household. It's okay, never stop praying. Open all the Prayer lines. Pray or World Peace.

CHAPTER 8

Let's step further into the mind of a Genius Invisible wall. A solid Foundation to look into the future. Every change will due to the chapter.

Equipped yourself with a safety net. Only our Faith can protect us from the unknown. This thought is given to all mankind. Not everyone will believe that there might be another world out there. The only thing I will say. Jesus owns everything and everyone in both Worlds.

Keep on walking this is just the beginning of an Avenue. Love without expectations, Find peace in every corner of life. A childhood dream will come to light someday. Faith holds the key to that door. Every country in the World will know what a Genius Invisible Wall is, for now it's just a book, that true Scientist or Special Doctors will find a loop hole that is up in the Air. Put them in a silent Room, give them a blank paper, let them write about this book. You would be surprise how many will see my future. Only the Gifted Soul will know the code to this Chapter. Remember that I can only see good in others. Use me wisely. an open mind will turn the lock. Success in hiding somewhere, if only you could deliver my message straight. Look deeper in your Faith, the answer is always there. This is not an easy chapter to understand. It could even be a quiz. Smile lets move on start climbing up the humanity Ladder.

Feed the poor, heal the sick, remember the homeless are all poems from my books. When I receive a very powerful dream that twist my membrane, I was sure Jesus was at his highest degree, when he gave me such dream. Genius Invisible Wall will be the Poet of the Nation.

When Married touch down into play mode. I will reveal more again. Your five poetry books will be apart of this package. You will never be in need of a Mentor again. Far from beyond the sky, I made this happen. Who am I?. Guess not keep on treading. Genius Invisible Wall will be no burden today or tomorrow.Everything is already on the table. Open your mind in the Universe, install Windows and doors, then open the windows and let the fresh Air in. This is a Nation that will judge from the best way possible, however not everyone will see eye to eye. Don't think too deep, just love every opinion with a grain of Salt. Add Sugar to test your Will. Smile with the Ocean Breeze. Nature is still in this plan. Faith, Family and Friends still hanging on a limb. Everyone culture is a different sentence. So allow Jesus to cross you over this stump. Genius Invisible wall will be mention in every Chapter keep your eyes open to see the change. Stay put, don't stop reading, at least, not just yet. The next line might be the only one you're waiting for.

Jesus loves you more than you can imagine. Never stop talking to him. His plan for you is stronger than you can think.

Feel your pulse, your Rate is getting higher. Be careful, you really don't want it to mess with your Blood Pressure. Wellness will take over this Chapter

Watch your weight could be embarrassing to read. Don't take it personal, I am talking to me. Smile this is now a work of Art. We're the Masterpiece with a wide range to grow, Believe it or not Faith is apart of this Daily plan. You need it without prescription. Chip in for free Meditation mentally they could walk hand in hand. File for an extra pass from Heaven not everyone will know what they're reading. Give everyone a clean slate. start over then re-enter this gate. Good Health is always a full Circle. Love every dizzy spell. recheck your courageous order. Read over again, just for extra points.

Play with your mind, it's almost possible if a Gifted Soul steps in this space. A new scale could save us time. Genius Invisible Wall first of its kind.

Order a scale without any numbers. Only a poem to recharge your perseverance, run for this invention might need an undercover. Let truth be told.

Everyday you could guess a new number, just before supper. Stay within your mindset. Just awhile longer. Take your Temperature for a tester.

Move on. Life is in a suspense Zone. No one will know the correct answer. This scale is now a member.

Oh boy I can feel exhaustion and tension setting in the mind of the Readers. Yet putting away this book could create an extra Chapter.Leave this line open for a test. Make yourself available to step out of your comfort Zone. Look deep in your Soul, what do you see?. Look deep in your Heart, what do you feel.

Find your Radial Pulse what do you feel? Peace and love is coming from me. Seek and you will find the true access to this dream. After all you could also be a Genius Invisible Wall. Only time will tell. Let's wait until the end. The Table is already made. Anyway there could still be twist and turns. Keep an open book filled with prayers. A guiding light to follow. A glimpse into the future. A Candle so bright, it turns off the lights. A unique way to see and feel the out of the ordinary clue. What a poor child to do. Someday this could carry a tune. Let's snap out of things and talk about life in America, in the next Chapter.

CHAPTER 9

Life in America is like a Merry go round. The Economy is any ones guess. The tide gets rough sometimes wearing a politics gear Corruption and Lies are still up in the Air. America and Jamaica are related in my eyes, I am still here. Mother and Son happy hour Giving and be the best one can be. Patois and English collides to make sense. It wouldn't be a sin if everyone graduate College.Life is fun and free. I hope that someday everyone in the World would own a Vegetable Garden, just to learn from the seeds. Then share the wealth for a learning experience. Make this happen, I wont be around forever. Education is still the number one gift to give a poor man child. I was a Farmers daughter, I am still not sure why he didn't want to be a good father. I would be the prettiest daughter created. at least that's how I would like to think. I wonder from time to time, what happen to my family tree in Jamaica. Everyone is all over the place.

I believe that when given the chance to learn, capture as many wisdom in abundance. save it for a Rainy day. get to the core of the learning ability that God created in you. For me Dr Lionel Mangue instilled good Diversity peace in me. When he sends me to America. See no color. Love Everyone watch your step, your Faith will kick in again for strength.

A poor man child will always love a challenge. Every child needs a pen and a blank paper to write down their ideas. Genius is in every head.

Focus is the passing grade to the end. A masterpiece is always waiting to re-enter the Brain. Think Big, think outside the box, if you can afford to read the end of the Clock. Think of the Root of the tree. Use the Stop Sign as a warning of the direction to take. Exploring on the Avenue that fits one personality trait. Creative mood swings on a limb to success. no need for distress in the land where freedom is not really free. Just believe in Faith without doubt. Giving freely is from the Heart. deep in the Wilderness could be fun. Wrap up in a Nature Blanket. Bond with everything beautiful. Everyone is a beautiful Walking family. America is own by God, only him can fully know the truth. Mankind will flip flop under my umbrella.

Genius Invisible Wall is related to five poetry books. Own the complete package. Someday Social Media will take over. I have more followers than my Publisher. This is a truth that could seem like a selfish cocky note. It's just confidence of a Gifted Soul. Learn from every angle.

Genius Invisible Wall is your free to call it what you want it to be. No one will judge not this time around. Find the poem that will match this journey. know the code, no need for a gurney. Life could be an emergency without burden. Think free when you think of me. I am not perfect, My English is

Weed out in my culture. No my dear, I do not smoke. Smile life could be a Prophet in the making. Only God knows. Jump into particles find something fun to do. Love yourself at the same level that you love others. Look in your Genius Mirror. See me at the same rate you can see yourself. Try not to sell me short. I will let you, but Jesus will punish you. It's just a Survival code. He's my mechanic, He's my Doctor. He's everything with wings. Please leave this line to fend for itself. America is a full pledge for all. Embrace your Faith in every corner of life. I can see you Hope. Leave this and press on to the future in America. Trials and tribulation will be everywhere. I will be dancing in the Rain with my no problem banner. My Roots knows the reason for my Gifted side. Neglect as a child, uplift by God. Lost my brother Solomon very early in life, yet he never leave my side. America is my Wings to fly.

Someday I will get ready to fit in my Poetry Dress, change the color and wear my Sunflower Gown, Get into my Red Wagon and leave everything behind.

Life is beautiful when everyone can see Gods plan. Wear creativity well, live it up like a Model. Find the Poem that uplift this Paragraph. You're a work of Art. You are a fisherman daughter. The core of this Gift could be complicated with the bare eyes. Get a method using a Scope. Testing is a way to read Genius Invisible Wall. It could work for everyone, if only you can figure it out. There will be no Barriers, get this straight. America is a Field to play in. Expand and invite the outside World for a view. Never judge this book by the cover. Inner beauty shines Daily with the Sun. Think Vitamin D fun. Smile for the camera.

CHAPTER 10

While the death of my Mentor sets in. I always remember his positive side. Everything could be funny and Goofy. It depends on what angle your'e viewing first. His demeanor was a Genuine Soul. He always wants to see me succeed and grow. I am sure he's in Heaven still helping other Angels and writing prescriptions for fun. His method to healing was simple. Spend as much time with your patient, until you can see their Hearts and Soul. Then balance the body to carry every burden. Every Household needs special attention, abundance of love to go around. Even though money alone cannot buy love. Ask the Doves. Somethings will always be missing, if you allow money to eat away your Soul. Balance light weight bearing on every shoulder. If you love someone set her free, if she doesn't return, well it wasn't meant to be. Smile someday you will understand me.

The Poorest child I send to College, will be the only one that remembers my name, when I am long gone. Someday you will repeat this again when you call my name. You might even tell your friends. Keep your circle small. Scope of Practice is everything. A code of silence is a good meditation piece.

Someday I will return and bring you flowers all over again. Read me a poem. My Genius Invisible Wall. You're the strongest woman I know. Should I take credit or should I let it go. Everything I did for you was from the Heart. No one could take your place. Your Velvet Teddy Bear was my Gift for you. Happy Birthday was the Happiest time of the year for you. I remember your beautiful smile. Why did you dedicated chapter ten for me. think deep. It's a reason.

A true best friend never dies, their memories will stay with you forever. They're like a family member. Keep on going be strong. Plug in your Faith everytime you want to sing your favorite song. I am everything because you love me. Real sparks for the Nation to twist. smile with every punches.

Live life like an Earth Angel, just like I trained you to do. See no color. remember every important Birthday. Love to the core, I will never leave your side.

The World is a dream away. You will own the Key to Success in the Future. Share your story with Oprah, after awhile everyone will see the change to America. The Gifted Soul will carry this change in the Genes. Everyone is a walking Poetry. Live to be free. Get to the family Tree. Leave a big gap for me.

Step in this Avenue like you owed it. Never see doubt or caption it. Two Geniuses, well I will leave this poem for you to read, think deep and read it over again, this is my belief. A Genius Doctor and a Gifted Child. One future in two body. Oh how scary. Now write your story enjoy every twist and turns.

Genius Invisible Wall could be written by me, Yet it's in the World published by you. One future no one saw coming. A book doctor will need to check all Blood Pressure, Normal when you look from the Window. Difficult to find the right cast. Your five books will guide you. Enjoy this Journey. Smile, a new Career will always welcome you. You're a true delight to work with. This cannot be contaminated by one jealous Supervisor. Smile and step over this experience. Turn it into a Half way Tree. Under the clock. Walk in your dreams. Success is knocking. Angels in Heaven rejoices for you. Send me a Heart Rhythm for this new system. Everyone is a winner, everyone is a star. Yet deep in the skies, enjoy true Geniuses. Ideas are born everyday. Gods Gift. Use it wisely to free the World. Faith Shelter and a lot of food to eat. Smile when you saw another Butterfly in your Garden, you never know this chemistry, it could be me.

CHAPTER 11

While the summary of my life brought poverty some suffering and pain. My Focus never leave the goodness of God. My Faith sets in and bail me out every time my Soul feels grey. The love I have for Jesus on the inside recharged on rainy days. My journey send waves and collapses in the wind. Look at me, I am still standing. My Terminology struggle to survive in the English world. Yet Jesus never forsake my Story. New growth sets in, I just got Married to my best friend Ralph, find the poem to collaborate this dream. His sister Evelyn was my best friend. Suspense is somewhere hiding. However God bless us well. My Invisible Wall went up when he ask me to sign a prenuptial agreement. I smile because I heard the conversation

I know the family member that was behind this doubt. Anyway Jesus knock everything out of the Ball game, So I wrote a visible poem for the World to read.

Justice of the peace was the way to say I do. It was God way of saying keep everything private. Too many negative force in this family. Every conversation you overheard, they said all Jamaicans are crazy. Life with Ralph is amazing. We are too private people, the only thing is, I write books for a living. He's owns his business in the Trucking industry. Driving is his hobby. He also love to rebuild his sport cars. I admire his strength and humble spirit. Life is looking up.

I am at a safe place, God knows exactly what I need in this World. He provided at no cost. True love from my Heart travels from New Jersey to Florida.

Everything that was missing in New Jersey God provides it in Florida. I challenge the nursing Assistant Test and pass. My Job in the medical field was very easy. This is all I know, how to help sick people, who needed me the most. Dr Mangue teaches me a lot of tender loving care. Hospice wasn't scary to me. Heavenly father has the final say. So I nurture patients back to health. Using motivation and encouragement. Comfort Care from Heaven.

Peaceful from a home setting, Again it's my believe that Faith can regulate every Heart Rhythm. True Love censored in to create circulation. Hospice is a man made material, oops I meant precaution. Not accurate. Only Jesus has the final call on expiration. Live life until it's time to visit Heaven. No ticket needed just repent of all sins. Heaven is an open book for everyone, Everyone will die one day. No more burden, no more pain, beautiful World to rebuild over again. we will call home Heaven.

All our Family and friends will be alive again. Paradise will be wide open to everyone dreams. A breakthrough is a Heart Rhythm on Earth, everyone is a break through in Heaven.

Masterpieces from every family Tree. Jesus will then bring out the Genius in me. Everyone will be reading my Poems. Then immediately turn them into songs. No more Diagnosis, everyone is wearing a healthy white suit. I walk Heaven looking for Dr Mangue, I look around and call his name.

Everyone is looking at me for a clue, I ask for his number 8769265883 up to this day, his number is the only one I could remember on Earth. Jesus said wake up my beautiful Angel. Everything here is apart of your 0400AM dream. I am not ready to return. Open A Poetry Workshop in every country, send your books to every family, uplift with one love, no boundaries, no Borders, No Walls. Faith will be the only answer. Life will be a Rainbow filled with beautiful colors.

Enjoy your Son and his children. Welcome his wife as your daughter. Enjoy your husband he's your soul Mate. Your Mother will be in Heaven someday. Pray for your broken family Tree. So much pain and secrets, floating in the winds. Forgiveness is on every door step.

Write for the Nation is a poem, make it happen. Write until the end of times, keep every one guessing. Keep Heaven Gates wide open. Don't worry your words are lined up with the Bible. Just be yourself. Yes it's okay to be different. Special, Gifted, share the same Faith. Keep an open mind. Always putting Jesus first page. Family is right there on the same page. Friends are in the numbers to read. Everyone can sow a seed. Drink from he same Fountain, Build a shelter Charity everywhere to help the poor. all your poems have a meaning.

Even a mobile Bookstore. Take time to read all your books. Collect the many Ideas.

Make all your dreams come through. Lifetime will pick up your story when you least expect it. Smile with the future. I am with you always, for true comfort.

CHAPTER 12

Genius Invisible Wall is a suspense Zone. Everyone is free to have their own opinion about me. It's more fun to see every aspect of your mind going to work. My open mind is large enough to love the World. My ability is far from your closet thoughts. Freedom lives within this circle, the square is also a perfect help. Everyone serves a purpose in my book. Jesus, gave me a Son, then he Blessed me with a Husband. My family Tree is still working hard to take a pinch out of me. Financially, I help my mother in Jamaica. My brother Solomon is my forever Guardian Angel, so is my Mentor Dr Mague forever he will live in my Heart.

You might not fully understand this masterpiece. Still put it in a frame. safe it for Mr Rainy day. Paid in full. All bills will be paid in Heaven. Smile, no more Tax collectors. Pastors will have no need to collect Jesus Tithes, everything will be taken care of. Life will be a happy center piece. Open to change to the color of the Rainbow. Faith will carry the truth. See everything Gods way. It's the correct path. Success is everywhere. Expand your Horizon to your full Potential. Poor is never a crime, It's not a sin. A rich Soul is given to all Man. Sow your seed well. Have respect for all women regardless of their Roots and culture.

When I am not around, Take care of my Son Edgar, give him a hug for me. I will someday be in Heaven with doggy Molly. Smiling and enjoy God Table

All Angels will know my name. One day, one sweet day, we will shelter under this universal umbrella of love. Everyone that did you wrong will repent.

Jesus will give everyone a clean slate. with three words on it.

Genius Invisible Wall.

Write your story for the world, then make me a sandwich for everyone in Heaven. Stop at Messenger Valley, Stop at Gifted Avenue, Search for Special Valley.

Make a U Turn on Genius Lane. Pray on Prophet Mountain, Meditate on Poet's Street. Your bond with Nature help to give you Wing. Your Tears were lined with Diamond. It's okay, you might not believe. Stay focus, I am reading Genius Invisible wall. Be my Mentor forever. This could be your suspense Zone. check your vital signs. Now watch me, I am gone with the wind. Dow Jones future, everything tied up with Nature. Storms Hurricanes, starts all over again.

I am watching from Heaven Gates. windows wide open with my hair blowing in the Wind. Everyone rejoice and sing. Jesus is Lord. A true GENIUS INVISIBLE WALL. No need to buy anything, everything here is free. Angels of wonders, welcome you.

GENIUS INVISIBLE WALL.

The Family Tree that's so broken
A child that learns to bond with
Nature from a very early age. A
Brother gone to Heaven too soon
Was a sad moment. A mother that rarely speaks because of
sorrows. Children dream to see a
Better Tomorrow. A sister that marry a pastor but never
looked back. Faith uplift from my angle.
Guided my step was Jesus rectangle. Set my path in a small
Circle. Search the World and find
The wisest Mentor glee. Then plug in Hope for a College
degree. Everything is a learning
Experience. Especially not growing up with a father. It so
Happen that my Earth Angel was
A real doctor. Call him my Mentor. I call him like a father.
Jump to America a different light.
Education is at everyone's door.
Supervisor hatred could send me
To the floor. Jesus uplifts me every time, I was face with
hostile environment. I moved on
I look ahead. My Gift will always be my Son. My smile
grows daily
From Gods love. Let's not forget my furry friend. Molly was
Send to me from Heaven. Now life is beautiful. God bless me
with a good Husband. True love
Will get us through any doubt.
The World will read then call Genius Invisible Wall a
Masterpiece.

Father God loves everyone in the World. You will sometimes feel alone, but Jesus is always with you. A supernatural feeling from Heaven.

Hurricane Irma was another challenge for the Gifted Child
Faith anchor us to safety.
Jesus leading the way.
Genius Invisible Wall source

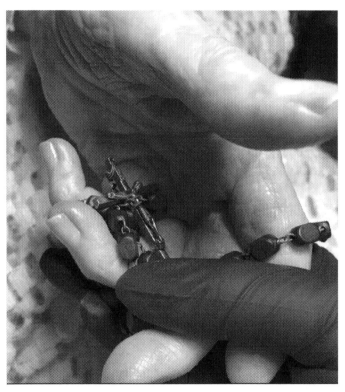

Genius Invisible Wall.
Faith always holds my hands.